DON'T GO BA   SLEEP

TIMOTHY LIU

saturnalia books

Distributed by University Press of New England
Hanover and London

©2014 Timothy Liu

No part of this book may be used or reproduced in any manner without written permission except in the case of brief quotations embodied in critical articles and reviews. Please direct inquiries to:

Saturnalia Books
105 Woodside Rd.
Ardmore, PA 19003
info@saturnaliabooks.com

ISBN: 978-0-9915454-0-7
Library of Congress Control Number: 2014945133

Book Design by Saturnalia Books
Printing by Westcan Printing Group, Canada

Cover art and inserts by Christopher Arabadjis.

Author Photo: Jimmie Cumbie

Distributed by:
University Press of New England
1 Court Street
Lebanon, NH 03766
800-421-1561

My thanks to the editors of *Asian-American Literary Review, The Bakery, Clade Song, Cobalt Review, Conversations Across Borders, Denver Quarterly, Four Way Review, Interim, Kenyon Review, Mandorla, The Margins, New South, Ocean State Review, Plume, The Progressive, Poetry Daily, Rattle, Seneca Review, Smartish Pace, Swink, They Will Sew the Blue Sail, Two Countries, Virginia Quarterly Review, Water Stone Review, Witness, Yale Review* and *Zocalo Square* for publishing these poems.

"The Lovers," "Unsleeping, 4:01 A.M.," "Unsleeping, 5:18 A.M.," "Unsleeping, 5:36 A.M.," and "Without You" first appeared in *The Thames & Hudson Project* (Fields Press, 2011) by Hansa Bergwall & Timothy Liu.

"The Remains," "The Silence" and "Classical Musical" will appear in *Two Countries: U.S. Daughters and Sons of Immigrant Parents.*

"The Decision" was reprinted in *Pushcart Prize XXXV: Best of the Small Presses* (Pushcart Press, 2011).

My thanks also to Bruce Beasley, Roberto Tejada, Henry Israeli, Jimmie Cumbie, Katie Rauk and Mason Gates for their close readings in the making of this book.

All the love in the world to my husband Chris and to my beloved Hansa.

This book is for my Tyger. Yld4e.

TABLE OF CONTENTS

"The love I talk of is not in the books."
—Kabir

A REQUIEM FOR THE HOMELESS SPIRITS

"There is no language to adequately describe the Japanese crimes."
—Ma Xiuyi, Survivor

Head of a Chinese soldier with a cigarette butt in its mouth
(taken by whom?) (given by whom?)
who never got to see the image he'd become
in the papers, in textbooks, online—

an image that has outlasted whatever grave
he did or did not get to have
in this life—

This is not how anyone would want to be remembered—

future generations thumbing through the pages, the files,
printing them out on desk-top printers, printing off

the same screens they use to check email, surf porn—

The winner of this contest will get his photo
on the front page of the paper,
the heads of Chinese men taken off
with one stroke of a broad sword

left nameless as a pile of rocks,

nameless as a headless corpse with hands bound
behind its back,
                    only the names of "the winners"
on the front page of the Nichi Nichi Shimbun

on December 13, 1937, in a language I cannot read
garlanding the photo of the smiling "winners"
in uniform, each propped up on his own sword—
an image someone else who knows the language
will have to explain to me—

And my hair stylist, Akiro, reads to me:

CONTEST TO KILL FIRST 100 CHINESE WITH SWORD
EXTENDED WHEN BOTH FIGHTERS EXCEED MARK—
MUKAI SCORES 106 AND NODA 105

Soon sleep will be taken away,
appetite taken away as that which clutches Akiro's throat
starts to spread—a cloud that began
from just two cigarettes a day,
no insurance for the eight hundred dollar price tag
attached to each procedure which may or may not save his life,
he who's already lost half of his voice, refusing
radiation for fear of losing
what remains, still recognizable as he takes an electric razor
to my scalp, sculpting something that will last
four weeks at best, he who's been doing this
for more than half his life, who tells me
he can still eat, still sleep eight hours a night
while handing me a card
for the next visit, a date that suddenly seems
further away than ever . . .

In a speech made in Nanking seven years after the Rape of Nanking,
Emperor Hirohito's youngest brother, Prince Mikasa,
detailed the extent of the military atrocities against the Chinese—

copies of his statement suppressed, buried
by the military authorities—

a single copy exhumed five decades later in the Parliamentary Library
by a Kobe University professor—

Order No. 119, Western Front Battle Operations, 16th Division,
20th Regiment, 1st Battalion, November 16, 1937:

ALL PROVISIONS TO BE LEVIED LOCALLY IN NANKING

(i.e. Rape, Loot, Pillage, Destroy)

And what do American textbooks say about First Nation genocide
beyond all those blankets laced with small pox?

And what will American textbooks say about Abu Ghraib, Guantánomo,
water boarding and extraordinary rendition fifty years from now

when History, as we all know, is written by "the winners"?

This is not how anyone would want to be remembered:
Rev. John G. Magee, chairman
of the International Red Cross Council,
racing through gunfire to rescue disarmed Chinese soldiers
being led off to the slaughter, Rev. John G. Magee
an amateur photographer who obtained a permit
from the Japanese authorities, the stills
from his 16mm movie camera largely responsible
for what we're able now to see,
his camera and film deposited at Yale
where he became a chaplain after the war . . .

Photos exist:

some were rounded up with barbed wire in groups of ten
and herded down by the river where the machine guns were waiting;
and some were forced to dig ditches, forced again
to lie down in them while the next group shoveled dirt
on top of them, muffling their screams,
others buried up to their necks
only to be beheaded, bayoneted, flattened by the treads of a tank;
some were burned alive, gasoline igniting communal pits.

Photos exist:

bayonet wounds on the back of a woman's neck
severing muscles down to the vertebral column,
some 80,000 women, ages 8-80, raped,
some of them stripped with their legs tied to a chair,
some passing out, others bleeding to death,
still others gang raped week after week
until they contracted venereal diseases
and were taken out to be shot,

objects inserted into the vaginas of corpses
before they were posed for photographs, the souvenir film
sent by Japanese soldiers to be developed in Shanghai
where extra prints were sometimes smuggled out
to news agencies across the ocean . . .

Memo to the 66th Regiment, 1st Batallion, December 13, 1937:

KILL ALL CAPTIVES.

Few of the survivors remain alive.
Few of the perpetrators remain alive.

Some of their stories have been recorded.
Many of their stories will never get told.

What should any of us do while they are still alive?

Akiro says:

Textbook revisions exist:

"Japan's *aggression* against northern China" replaced with
"Japan's *advance* into northern China."

"Japan's *invasion* of South East Asia" replaced with
"Japan's *advance* into South East Asia."

Please discuss.

MUKAI SCORES 106 AND NODA 105.

The newspaper article a fabrication, *a complete fiction*,
Mukai's attorney said before the War Crimes Tribunal,

propaganda that made for an enticing story for the two
instantly famous lieutenants to seek out new brides . . .

And when the Japanese police showed up at Mukai's door
in the spring of 1947, Mukai said, "I did nothing wrong,"

telling his wife that the killing contest was all made up.
"Oh, then, you lied to me!" his wife reportedly said . . .

Baskets of gold, baskets of jade:

how can we trust the testimony of survivors
not to be exaggerated?

Baskets of gold, baskets of jade:
all of it left behind, my mother said,
when the Japanese marched towards the gates
of Nanking, my mother born in 1936
according to the lunar calendar,
never quite sure which date to officially use
on her California driver's license,
my mother's family who went from everything
to nothing, baskets of jade, baskets of gold
hauled off by soldiers overnight . . .

but something's not quite right,
my father says, about the time and the place;
she was born in Xian, not Nanking,
she wasn't even there when the soldiers
scaled the walls after dropping ordnance
sun up to sun down for weeks on end;
something must be wrong with her medication . . .

though it's true, my father says,
her family ran from the Japs, we all did,
just not in 1937. You know how she gets
everything *confused*. Baskets of jade,
baskets of gold, my mother in and out

of psych wards for the last decades
of her life, dead at the age of 62,
half a globe and more than half

a century away, no way to verify
exactly what she meant when she pulled
a long gold hair from her own scalp

and said: You know, you must be at least
an eighth German, but your father . . .

so many things he still doesn't know.

Canceling class, I stay home from school,
order three DVDs online
and surf the web all day for atrocities:

- horse urine injected into human kidneys
- animal blood injected into veins
- sea water injected into veins
- air injected into veins
- bubonic plague injected into veins
- limbs amputated then reattached to opposite sides of the body
- flamethrower practice
- vivisection without anesthesia
- limbs frozen off till only a torso and head remained, still breathing, eyes open

When my brother brought his girlfriend home
for the first time, he thought her being Asian
and a member of the college speech team

would be enough. But when my parents heard
her last name had a few syllables
too many—Horiuchi, Yamaguchi—whatever

it was, what could they do but frown
and whisper to one another: *she's Japanese—
so vicious.* My family no longer knew

which country each of us were living in . . .

Canceling class, I stay home from school,
trying to square the accounts of just how many
were massacred: 300,000? 200,000? 50,000? 50?

Very little remains
of the first grade,
only Sherri
on a jungle gym
at recess chanting
*milimated monkey
meat, roasty-
toasty parakeet,
wormy vomit
flowing down
the avenue and
now it's time for
lunch, I forgot
my spoon!* That
and one other:
*Chinese, Japanese,
Hercules, look
at these!* as Sherri
rocked back and
forth, bodacious
knees churning
inside an oversized
tee. Never asked
her why she pulled
the outer corner
of her eyes up
for Chinese and
down for Japanese.
Quite sure now
even she didn't
know how such
pieces of rote
performance art

got handed down
at recess, the source
of their origins
unknown, at least
to us, in 1971.

And before they knew it, they found themselves
beyond what they thought they were

capable of—bayoneted survivors who felt they had
no choice but to bring their trophies home—

Japanese heads impaled on long bamboo poles.

Little else remains from my sophomore year
in college but a course in Abnormal Psych,
and little remains of that except for a lecture
the professor gave about a serial killer
who used to roam the Timpanogas Mountains
on the very trails we were likely to hike as soon
as school got out. Said the thing the killer
liked to do most after binding his victims'
wrists and ankles with duct tape was to
turn on a portable cassette recorder while he
chose one of many possible blades from
a Swiss Army knife his mother had given him,
curious how the wounds he inflicted would
each produce a different sound as the blade
went in, then out, he who'd make an archive
of his research, documenting the difference
between puncturing a kidney versus a liver,
an eyelid instead of a spleen, and the relish
our professor took imitating some of the screams
he'd heard began to trump the facts themselves,
he who had become the very thing he knew
so much about, and in so doing, made
the lesson all the more memorable, indelible.

Inscription on the Tombstone of the Homeless Spirits:

In October of 1938, I (Gao Guanwu) was instructed by the government to go to Nanking. It was a year after the Nanking Incident. Remains, however, still could be found on the mountains, at the city walls, in the thick growth of grass and along the rivers. I myself collected 2,600 remains in the city and buried them. Two months later, the villagers related to me that there were more abandoned remains at Maoshan, Maqun, Ma'an and Ling Gu Monastery. The villagers pleaded for burial of those remains. Therefore I conveyed this matter to the Public Health Bureau. As a result, more than 3,000 bodies were collected and buried at the Ling Gu Monastery. This monument was erected to guard against wild beasts and to memorialize those homeless spirits.

This text is from a rubbing. The stone is now lost.

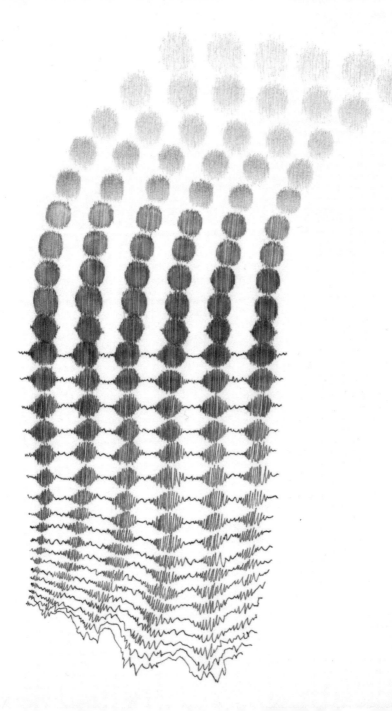

BUILDING TRUST

I liked it when he fucked me
when I was half asleep
as if I were a pot of coffee
he was used to putting on
before anyone else in the house
got up. Give him whatever
the hell he wants, my mother
said with shiners in both eyes,
heirloom Limoges smashed
on kitchen tile. The body
of my mother being rolled
into the morgue's gas jets
is what I picture whenever he
enters me, knowing I can't
bring myself to visit her grave,
not once. It would be
the most disingenuous act,
my therapist says, who knows
her only through stories
that I've told, most of them
lies. I actually don't
like it when he fucks me
with skirt hiked past my hips
and our hour isn't even up,
his impatience something
I'd rather deal with
off the clock, otherwise
what am I paying him for—
surrogate father who fucks
me better than my own father

ever did, who spares me
the command to look into
his face with blackened eyes
as he comes, knowing I can't
be trusted, not by anyone.

THE DECISION

When I removed

the ring I had
been wearing for

a decade, a ghost

ring remained
underneath—the skin

slightly paler

where the gold
had been—my finger

cinched where it

had been constricted
as I prepared to

step into the night—

I KNOW MY HUSBAND'S BODY

I know my husband's body
better than anyone else, especially
the way he likes to be entered
with my thumb depending on
the weather. In our eighteen years
together, I've made him come
well over a thousand times, most of it
in our first year. He cups my balls
and knows exactly how long it's been
since I last came, teasing me about
being more faithful to my own hand
than to his. There's a man
whose body I may never know
who knows *his* boyfriend's body
better than anyone else, a man
who's closer to me than anyone I know,
the two of us having vowed to keep
our clothes on. I must confess
I'm usually the first to rise, to shit
the semen out and shower off
before crawling back to bed
where my husband snores till noon
only to enter me again—this being more
than anyone would want to know
except for the man who wants
my body more than my husband could
possibly know. Is it worse
to imagine what another's body will
or will not do? I know a woman
who thinks her husband is someone else

every time she opens her legs,
careful not to cry the wrong name
as my father did inside his new bride
on their first night—my mother's
ashes in an urn above their headboard.
It was never about technique.
There's no manual for any of this.
So get behind the wheel and drive.
There are places in our bodies
no one has ever reached—

THE ASSIGNATION

Every vow I kept
for twenty

years I wanted to
keep right up

to the moment
my finger slipped

inside of him—

ROMANCE

He makes me feel
too much. Don't care
if he's already married,
if his spouse knows
how to lick bone china
clean. As if everything
stunk of meat. I wait
on the curb for someone
to explain why it feels
so wrong to be here
with a plastic bag over
my head, not knowing if
I have a name, not unless
he calls—his voice
barreling down on me
like an ice cream truck
with its pre-recorded
Pavlovian song ringing
while I play dead in
the middle of the road
and I have no pocket
change, no job, how is it
he makes me feel
like I'm nine years old,
like I haven't yet come
inside a sleeping bag
filled with feathery down
as I rub against another
boy, my asshole sore
from fingering myself
without him knowing.

DREAM FRAGMENT ON THE EVE OF MY BELOVED'S WEDDING

Came into a field of dry grasses
beside a grotto, mountain lions

tense and lithe, one basking
on a boulder in full sun, the other

circling underneath, and then
they were gone—two creatures

who didn't belong to anyone—

WITHOUT YOU

I was doing just fine, a job, a home,
a life—a salt shaker on the table
in some museum not visited in years

Didn't know that I was waiting

Didn't know if I was even awake

Without you I am the diorama's
glassed-in air, the dew drop
that never falls in a time-lapse photo

Of all the empty tables in my favorite
cafe, why did you have to seat yourself
next to mine, taking away a view
I'll never get back?

Without you I'm a tray of coffee mugs
the waitress spills in slow motion
on the night she got fired

"Very expensive coffee" my mother
said for the rest of her life

My mother who sleeps in an urn

Without you I am a lie a child tells
for the very first time

Without you I touch myself and feel
my hand grow alien and strange

Who doesn't feel curious muscles
when exploring their own holes

Without you I am the sound
of a tinkling cymbal and empty brass

Love whomever, then return

For without you, I'd have forgotten
the many doors through which
the world disappears—

THE RING

How long before the grave
claims what is mine
and the ring is removed
from my hand—a gift
whose provenance remains
unknown—scratches
and nicks the only clues
as to where it's been? Ring
my husband will strip off
my finger before I ride
into the morgue's gas jets.

I KNOW YOUR MOUTH BETTER

I know your mouth better
than your husband ever will.

Every time he kisses it,
your mouth disappears

a little more—the passion
spent on nailing boards

that keep your house from
falling apart. You and I

have no house, only these
two mouths between us—

our past unkissed, our future
flooding into those streets

where nothing else stands.

A LOVER DOESN'T HAVE TO

call you back. Think of the Sufis

who chose God for a lover. Think
of the Virgin Mary who chose

her Only Begotten. Think of Christ

who chose his own Father who
abandoned him in his darkest hour

which we all know about. Christ

enthroned in heaven now sitting
next to his Father, their hands

never touching. As your friend

I must confess each time we get
together, I can't help but imagine

you swinging in a leather sling,

legs trapezing above my head as I
kneel on the floor, my fingers

wet with lube, curling into a fist.

IF EVERYTHING I SAID

were a lie, if all I wanted
was to pick your brain
or suck you dry and then
make off with your baby
destined to be a king,
you too would walk away
from me without a second
thought, you said, certain
I'd agree that it was all
a sham, myself lost
in thought the moment
you hung up, remembering
a friend I knew in college
who made me take a vow
inside a Mormon Temple
that we'd know each other
for the rest of our lives,
that whoever died first
would be waiting to greet
the other on the other
side of the veil, the closest
friend I'd ever had up until
that moment I decided to
come out to him. Bob.
Whose father broke his
mother's nose in seven
places, who dislocated
her shoulder twice because
he was in the mood, moving
out of the house only when
Bob and his three brothers
cornered him with a shotgun

in their garage, this story
told to me through tears
a decade after the fact.
Bob, whose stepfather climbed
into his bed, into each of his
brother's beds, only this time,
no one said a word, in fear
of breaking up another
marriage. Bob who said
to me: "Everything between
you and me is a lie: sharing
the same room, showering
at the gym, staying out
or up until dawn, all of that
means something different
now." It didn't matter
that I never touched him
in a place that would've made
him jump. Bob, who moved
to Arizona, who didn't stay
in touch, though I heard
he was getting married,
just couldn't bring himself
to send an invitation.
Everything wasn't a lie.
Another decade passing by.
Perhaps I am still a fool
waiting. Bob. Whose son
I've never met answers
the phone and tells his dad
an old friend is on the line.

ROMANCE

His body wasn't terribly abused.

More like a copy of a used book
bought online with very minimal

marginalia scrawled in pencil

by its previous owner who lost
interest after the first few pages—

something one can easily erase.

THE GIFT

When his hands were on
the wet clay turning
on the wheel, I did not ask

what he was shaping,
whether it was for flowers
or wine. It was only after

he took his hands off
and fired what he'd made
in the kiln that I knew

what I was without him.

A BED OF ASH

still warm to touch. I scavenge it
for chunks of charred wood to be used

as quick coals to get the next fire

going. Some people hit the bottle.
I turn off my phone to intensify

the pain. Convince myself that when

I power back on, there won't be
any messages. My mother died twice:

once when her body was burned

and again when her phone was
disconnected—me calling just to hear

a voice say: "The number you dialed

is not in service." The man who left
my bed this morning has not returned

my calls. And if I bury my phone

in the woods out back? Before he left,
he asked if I ever felt lonely here,

and I said, of course not, I'm a writer.

THE GIFT

Had the kind of smile abuse
survivors had, a kind of smile
that turned me on. Was used
to prefacing his disclosures
with "never actually told this
to anyone before," meaning
everyone else in the room
had probably heard. So adept
at keeping us from talking
to one another about secrets
that he told, it became more
difficult to tell exactly who
the abusers were, which one
of us had done those things
that left those scars. It was
what drew me in, the chance
that I could be the one who did
this thing to him even if we
had hardly met, that I could do
this thing that had been done
to him, only better, inflicting
an even deeper wound than
the one he'd sustained, the one
he made me promise never
to disclose. That much we had
in common, this confidence
we shared. Fucking him over
a pleasure, knowing the way
I'd be remembered was to
hurt him all the more, beyond

what he believed had been
the limit. I would take him
there, over and over, only
asking that he try to keep it
a secret between us, knowing
that this in fact was the gift
he'd never keep to himself—

ROMANCE

Like an explosion in a pickle
factory. Like an addict
shoveling a snowbound
driveway with a coke spoon.
Like a pair of clean socks
he puts on only after racing
through a thunderstorm
with one sneaker on.
Like a bull's-eye, a beehive,
scrambled eggs and brains
he can only get at Nadine's
in Salt Lake City and only
if he orders whatever's not
on the menu—my favorite
daily special, my mouthful
of crushed ice, my alpha
and omega locomotive
barreling down the tracks
where I lay spread eagle
with a thermos full of pisco
steeped in nettles, lips
parched, hips bruised,
and the world all atilt,
drunk on nuptial cocktails
with a splash of bitters,
no sperm facial ushering in
the morning-after mudslide
of his ravished looks, don't
worry, cause I'll be just fine
without him, without his

two-stepping savior-faire
whisking me off my feet
and up the bridal stairs
to an antique four-poster
bed missing a post, a gimp
honeymoon spent on
a busker's dime, a frat boy's
beer-soaked fart, so sick
of his speculative talk as he
pumps my pussy as if I
were the Tour de France
on steroids, no telling what.

THE CRISIS

You take the call at three a.m.
and it's your boss who says
she's staring at a bottle of pills

so you ask if she feels alright
and the next thing you know
she's at your door, asking if

she can take a shower, only to
reappear wearing your robe
as she slides down next to you

on your sofa bed, giving you
no choice but to run out for
smokes at the corner bodega

then pound on a buddy's door
who says of course you can
crash—a bottle of bourbon

sloshing in his lap, his woman
out of town—a giant plasma
screen streaming live gay porn.

ROMANCE

You went to bed not knowing
someone would hurl a skunk
through the window you left

open. If you close your eyes,
will everything simply turn
back into a dream—the safe

un-cracked, towel strips
soaked in kerosene not
stuffed down your throat

while the neighborhood din
dies down? How many kids
did the newscast say it took

to overturn that armored car
parked outside your door,
your body a cash machine

waiting to be fed—the dirt
and grease from countless
strangers poking, demanding

you give them what they
want while animal control
looks the other way, unable

to explain why their traps
remain un-sprung, why the sun
looks more like a moon you

left behind one summer night
at camp—the sheets thrown
off your bed while someone

below scaled up your peaks,
knuckles gripping crevices
as he hoisted himself up

and over, leaving a stench
not even a tub of tomato juice
could wash off is what you'd

tell your shrink if only you
could afford it, credit scores
damaged beyond all repair.

THE LOVERS

You are the angry valentine
and the envelope I cut
my tongue across while sealing
its flap shut. You are
the bumpy rash spreading
across my shoulder at four a.m.
and the tab of Claritin
dissolving in my blood—
a forgotten dream
that nags at me off and on
throughout the day,
a pyramid of crystal
goblets stacked on top
of one another downstairs
at the Crate and Barrel
a stone's throw from where
you work because you
needed to get away.
If only I had a magnum
of Dom Perignon, I'd
pour ebullient waterfalls
to rival the fountains
at Versailles. You won't
be going home to your wife
tonight, not while an elephant
charges across the floor
with gleaming tusks
where herds of panicked
post-holiday shoppers duck
behind those see-through

plastic curtains with mermaids
undulating through them
while you crouch low in some
out-of-the-way corner with
a Blackberry at your ear
listening to my voice—you
who never much liked talking
without being able to see
my face, o my Chevalier,
my hillside of flat stones
piled high on the outskirts
of Châteauneuf-du-Pape,
my hot plate of used corks
glued together from all the meals
we've shared, the teapot
whistling whenever you found
your way to my table,
I of such little faith
in your love for me, in love
with me while spinsters
plump the nuptial bed
with the plucked feathers
of outsized swans—pillows
I'll never get the chance
to lay my head upon
or dream upon, won't you
forgive me of my greed,
my wayward imaginings
of a life other than the one
we are given only once,

your voice pounding
in my ear, in consort
with my heart as if we
were post-coital lovers
conversing in the dark
while shadows flit about
the honeymoon suite,
its air perfumed with roses
in a cut-glass vase identical
to the one my mother
kept in her childhood home—
dragons swirling on a silk
drawstring bag drawn shut
with tassels made of gold—
nineteen beads of lapis lazuli
dangling on her wrist her man
never asked about, not once,
in all their years of marriage—
such passions fully spent.

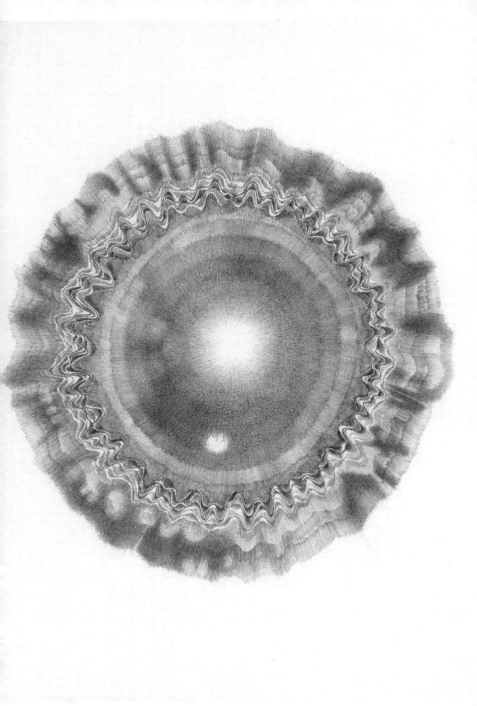

FIRST MEMORY

My mother in a stupor,
stumbling down

the hallway in panties
soaked in blood—

my hand leading her
back to bed.

CLASSICAL MUSIC

On the day my mother died, I unplugged
the stereo at a time when record clubs
still sent out their selections of the month

unless you said otherwise. The mail piled up
on a table in the entry hall—an avalanche
of bills and condolences I knew I didn't

have to respond to. People would understand.
My cat stopped sitting on the amplifier,
found other sources of heat to get through

a winter punctured by the clang and hiss
of radiators built before my mother was born.
Feeding the cat, changing the litter—done

without music in the house. Months later,
I took myself to a live concert, something
by Mozart, something I remember first

having heard in the back of a '68 Rambler,
the radio on, my mother and father trying
to guess the name of the composer, the one

game I knew my mother would win. It comes
to that. One moment you're turning a dial
lit up on the dash, and the next, you're not—

ANOTHER ANXIETY ATTACK

As the lights in the theater dim before they actually dim.

So the price-gouged profits of war-torn Iraq.

Hiatus or terminus too soon to tell.

Withholding control.

The indefinite wait as substitute for any real news.

Pain or hurt not part of the equation.

Yet the rescue! The story!

Having thought a simple kiss might obliterate his past.

Romance as replacement therapy.

The paramour as the resuscitated mother.

My mother's heart a lemon.

A real clunker.

A tyranny of thwarted ambitions.

Like a desert where nothing lush could grow.

Imagined oasis lending access to a wished-for not there.

THE SILENCE

She took the spareribs out of the oven
and set them steaming on a plate
before leaving her apartment.
I didn't know how long to wait,
tore into cold meat when I decided

my mother wasn't coming back.

*

No one knew about the gun she kept
in her purse until the authorities
called—a .38 caliber pistol
with a pearl handle and a trigger
even she could easily pull—
her car still waiting to be towed
from a roadside ditch

when they arrived on the scene.

*

Yesterday morning, I was leaning
over a kitchen sink, my husband
upstairs sleeping. Between his snores
muffled under a down comforter
and a portable electric heater that kept
our bedroom warm, I knew
I could sob as loud as I wanted

without disturbing his dreams.

*

At the sports arena between musical acts
and clouds of dope, I texted my lover
a wide-angle shot of the stage—
the reception bars on my phone
bouncing back and forth between high
and low—a text I had to send
several times before it went through
even though there was a chance
his phone would be off or the text get
lost for hours in the ether, even days.

The silence is the agony.

*

My therapist says: *It's not your fault.*
No way for you to have known
exactly where your mother was headed.

Then why am I left weeping
in my kitchen decades after the fact?

When I went upstairs and sat
beside my husband, he could feel
the mattress shift beneath our weight
even though I felt much lighter
after watching translucent ropes of snot
lowering down into the sink, arms
around me when I asked if he

was awake, knowing that he wasn't.

*

How many romances get derailed
when a text that has been sent
fails to go through? How many mothers
disappear through a kitchen door
never to return—the food on the table

the last meal they will ever serve?

*

My lover texted back: *where are you now?*
Having no idea what I'd been
going through when he texted again:

Wish I was there with you.

DEEP SONG

I lost the road

awhile back—
you the rock

come to smash

my compass
(didn't I ask

for it, didn't

you warn me
not to get in

your way) you

the road I lost
awhile back—

you who left

me nothing
but wilderness

to sing through.

ANONYMOUS

A streak
of moth dust

left on the wall

where a hand
had been—

HERE

in the building where you take
the anonymous test, everything is
neutral, the lights overhead
repeating rows of honeycombed
fluorescence intermittently
abuzz, one tube flickering on
and off, unable to decide if
the men here are all here
for the same test. It took you
more than fifteen years to mark
the box *same-day result,* the box
you first misread as *re-slut,*
and though you are partnered,
you went to your appointment
alone. Perhaps it is melodramatic
to dwell on a test thousands
take everyday, but then you think
of the thousands who don't,
preferring *not to know*
the consequences of the choices
they have made even if
the ones they've lusted after
hardly seemed a choice. And whose
was the voice who answered
your call and scheduled you in
the way any receptionist
or out-call body worker would?
Think of the high your neighbors
got each night while playing
Take Five or the Mega Millions

jackpot, how sometimes you too
gave in to impossible odds,
but who hasn't had such fantasies
over a single life-changing
moment everyone can make
themselves party to, you wonder
on your way to the clinic
while passing the bodega's
magic-markered sign now up
to 145 million as you reach
into your pocket for any change,
asking yourself if today might
be the day you'll finally get
what you deserve, the chairs
in the waiting room now mostly
empty, you with the last
appointment, the other men
having walked out of the room
with band-aids at the crooks
of their elbows, already having
spelled their answers out
in blood, adrenaline pumping
at the starting block as you wait
for the gun to go off, not yet
knowing what will rule the day
this time around, only the steps
you took which led you here—

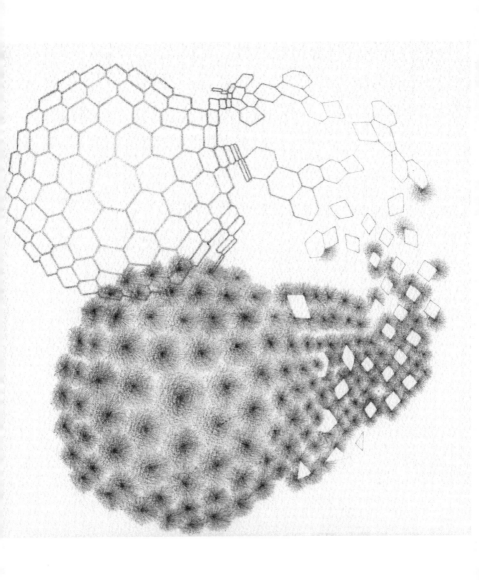

UNSLEEPING, 3:25 A.M.

Whatever you do, don't go
back to sleep. I know you spend
your waking hours making sure

everything's in its proper place
even if you throw a tantrum
when you bump into a chair—

disorder brought into your home
where the furniture remains
the same but the room itself

is altered. Don't go back to sleep:
I've waited all my life to cross
your threshold and wake you

from your slumber—your body
sealed under glass waiting for
an axe un-hewn by human hands—

and in that instant you finally
awake, I too feel the cleaving
go right through me, the future

stripped of its past in a place
I've never been but through your
eyes—so don't go back to sleep.

ROMANCE

The uncorked bottle waiting
to lead us into five uneven
glasses of Bordeaux because
you are you and I am nothing
but the cheapest kind of date
still able to hold his own if
only given a chance to show
I know the difference between
a Pauillac and a Margaux
as each decants into a steeper
plumminess hinting at chewy
game, you who could care
less what grapes are grown
on which side of the river—
a jug of Gallo, a box of Rosé
really all the same, never mind
the vintage just so long as it
pleasures us, my face already
flushed, my eyes past tipsy
zooming in on the moist end
of the cork set down where
you last fingered it, oblivious
as to whether a château has
Grand Cru status or not, happy
to know that you can trust
my taste, that if I say "traces
of lead, wild grass on the nose,"
your tongue will find its way
into my mouth, the bottle
drained to its sulfitic dregs.

WITHOUT ASKING

I pluck the maraschino
out of your Manhattan—
tie the stem into a knot
with my tongue, feel that
charge when you grab
the burnt uneaten toast
off my breakfast plate
in a redneck Catskills
bakery and shove it in
your mouth when it's clear
you've had enough to eat
but still want something
on the side—compote
smeared across your lips
the secret held between us
while everyone else closes
out their tabs, tips their
servers generously or not,
unaware how things go on
right under their noses
all the time, the way you
twirl my Pilot G2 pen
round and round, clicking
the ball point in and out
before pocketing the thing
I thought didn't belong
to you—telling me how
poppers dull the meat
that sometimes punishes
your hole, numbs the ache
you don't want taken
away, not without asking.

UNSLEEPING, 4:01 A.M.

if you tied a blindfold around my head
and led me to the very edge

if you offered me bruised fruit

if you chained me to a rock
would I still sing out

every one of your given names

especially the one you hate

until you saw it fit to cut my throat
pry off the shield

soldered to my chest

my cocksure strides unhorsed at last

my body mud enough for the gods
to walk upon

my eyes but luminous stones
to mark your path

all the way back down

THE CRUSHING DIN

By evening, my hearing
has worsened. I can smell them—
the bats in the caves behind my cottage

stirring. A fungal rust
creeps along the edges of pines
at full summer. Not a single car all day

has passed where I sit naked
on a screened-in porch.
Nor has a neighbor stopped by in a year.

The expiration date stamped on my tin
of imported tea is past its date
but when does tea go bad, I think, inhaling

the steam that rises off my mug.
When was the last time I saw the flag
on my mailbox raised? Only ants

march up and down the post
each morning when I walk out to the curb.
One day, I won't be coming back.

THE WINDOWS

The windows are turning pale
in a room where I sleep beside a man
who does not believe I love him
anymore, the same pale light
that lifted me out of sleep
in an Edinburgh room—stuffed
armadillo on the bureau, heel
hooked around my shin, your chin
cradled in the crook of my arm—
hunger's monotonous engine
humming its tune in pre-dawn light
where a Victorian duvet fell
five time-zones away where you
still are, your students mired
in exams when I flew back home
in an exit row, an aisle seat,
the windows too bright against
sleep's deficit that had accrued
on holiday while we were crossing
borders—switching trains
at Newcastle, the tracks ahead
closed off, cutting cross-country
to Carlisle over verdant landscapes
stippled with sheep, my eyes
darting back and forth from you
back out to a world beyond the glass
I'd miss each time my focus
returned to you—a detoured train
getting us where we thought we
needed to be going . . . what remains
is a piece of woven Peruvian string

tied against my wrist, a bracelet
that loosens now a little more
each day I walk down to the pier
to a skyline you have never seen,
thinking of that other piece of string
tucked under your jacket sleeve
as you chalk the board, light
pouring in through the windows
when I dashed into Ellis Brigham
two minutes before they closed,
lying to the security guard
about a jacket that was "being
held" for me, my wallet so fat
with cash, would he please
just let me in? and just because
you weren't right there, was that
any less real than a squadron
of zippers stitched into waterproof
seals running zigzag across a bomber
jacket you still wear? It's 9:42
and you're sitting exams, me naked
with a man who's shared my bed
for nineteen years, who doesn't know
whom I love, and I'm wide awake
fingering a worn piece of string,
dreaming about a Newcastle pint
you and I once swigged as we walked
on that road to Leith, the windows
turning pink at sundown, the two of us
hardly knowing where we were
headed, only that we were going—

ALL TRAINS ARE GOING LOCAL

Slowing down your body enough to feel.

Thought you were at a standstill
but you were only slowing down enough

to feel the pain. There are worse things

than running to catch the train, twisting
your ankle, the afternoon fucked.

Running to get to or away from?

the stranger who helps you up
wants to know, you who are so used to

anything scribbled on a prescription blank.

Just want the pain to go away, you say,
surprised to find yourself

reaching for someone else's hand.

EASY DOES IT

He works all summer

and won't think twice
about taking me

into his mouth, says

he has as much feeling
for me as he does

an Eskimo Pie, could

plow through a box
in a single afternoon

if it were hot enough—

THIS TOO SHALL PASS

You think of the time
a stranger put his
fingers inside of you

at the back of a bus,
smearing a little blood
on the seat next to yours

when he got off—a man
who didn't even ask
your name. No one talks

about what lingers on
in the mind, whether
everything went faster

or slower than you
wanted, only knowing
it's more than over.

THE GARDEN OF EARTHLY DELIGHTS

Either eat the thing
or don't. Either unhinge
your jaw and take in
this world or leave it

alone. Such a simple
thing, what one is willing
to put in one's mouth
or not. I wanted you

to be changed, to feel
the slow piston of what
I was moving through
what I longed to say

but couldn't. Some say
I was wrong for wanting
this. Others couldn't
start to censure us fast

enough, said I was like
a contagion, the pox
on you is what they kept
on saying. People say

all sorts of things but
was the thing prepared
to your liking, satisfying
what you had imagined

all your life? I was not
confused, could see
beyond the moment's
repast into the cold

everlasting. Love gets
down on all fours
and straddles the thing
it loves, and just like that,

it's over. The hunger
moves on to whatever
comes next, the bottle
uncorked, the night

unfurling its little wings
that lift our heels up
into the air as we recline
on a couch that pulls out

of Dodge, no evidence
left behind. That's how
we've always wanted
to leave this world.

THE ASSIGNATION

You said: come outside—
all the planets are still in the sky.
I wanted to linger awhile

longer—dawn's champagne light
drowning out whatever there was

to be seen: books that fell
off the shelves in the latest quake
lying face down on the floor.

We knew what thoughts to write
in the thought balloons floating

above our heads, only didn't know
how to start on the animation
and get ourselves beyond

deadlines. A sprained ankle kept us
from a world that didn't want

to wait. Couldn't remember where
the car was parked, only fishnet
stockings dusted with glitter

left on those bucket seats reclined
back as far as they could go—

THE BETROTHAL

I am standing at the altar
ready to flee. Never
has fidelity been so easy
on a body that knows how to

pleasure itself. No wonder
marriages are duller than
grunts rising from the rear
of shag-carpeted minivans.

No wonder your mouth runs
over me like a Mustang
through a thunder storm
with the top down, my hair

standing up on end, my tongue
doing push ups in my throat
as it tries to get in shape.
Forget about bands of gold

when there are holes enough
for every last finger. Chew me
to the new moons. Show me
stars only lovers can see

on the flats of their backs,
sirens in the distance
scraping against our ears
like a gravedigger's shovel

left on the steps of a church.

ROMANCE

We stand in line for
a pack of cigs, my man
who lets me drag off
his rather than giving me
my own. Some say
he's never slept with
another man. Driving
home, my hand rests
on his when he's done
shifting, as we listen
to someone croon:
It was the first time
& you knew you would.
And his SUV turns
into a boat of flowers
nosing into waves
of wheat just off
the Interstate—forty-five-
dollar-a-night motel
rooms inviting us
to stop pretending there
isn't a whole lot more
going on. All I know
is I miss him all the time
when we're not bathed
in dashboard light,
everything I could want
right there—a man
I know I could leave
my husband for,

the ring on my finger
a shackle, a trifle,
no road long enough
for where we're headed.

SUMMERTIME

His cock inching up my spine
vertebra by vertebra
as he pulls my shoulders tighter
against his chest, then his
mouth making sucking noises
down my back as if his
ambition were to somehow
blow himself.
        So I ask him
what I smell like, I who want
to wrap my body in the tongue
of a man who recites Rilke
in the original, I who have grown
so tired of translations getting
in the way like the thinnest
lambskin sheath
              and he says:
You smell like summertime—
like flies on the windowsill
fucking while the blades
of a ceiling fan turn inside
a room where a ten-year-
old boy has just come for
the first time—underpants
thrown to the floor—a virgin
musk the world has failed
to bottle.
        Of course I'll leave
my scent on his sheets,
wondering when he'll do

the wash, just in time
for the next one to arrive
and give him what I know
I can't—the season's fickle
indolence magnified by
the voice of a woman singing
the blues decades after
she's gone.
        No one dies
in the summertime, he says
off the cuff, something I want
to be true even if I know
winter's just around the corner—
a face cord of fragrant wood
needing to be stacked even if he
won't ask—his body alone
telling me exactly what to do.

THE BRIDEGROOM

He said: *you talk too much.*
He said fucking his wife
was like doing the stations
of the cross, over and over,
always in the exact same
way. He told me to saddle up
my ponies, told me to go
easy there, hoss, his voice
a blindfold around my head.
I did exactly what he said.
He liked my thick hair, liked
squeezing my mouth slowly
open with finger and thumb,
prying down my lower lip
before gently grazing there.
Soon after he stopped
saying anything, his hand
holding up the backside
of my head, cradling it like
a newborn calf, his hardness
riding against my loins,
crushing my sex, the bruises
only showing later as proof
of his sudden visitation—
late afternoon sun starting
to dip below the ridge,
the sky itself tuning from
champagne to cinnamon,
his body all vice and torque
as he took me in his arms,

bride and chattel, his tongue
a branding iron that took
its time, burning the moment
into me, a wetness already
pearling there, his eyes
scratching out the prayers
I knew by heart, I who knew
there'd likely be nothing
left when he got through.

UNSLEEPING, 5:18 A.M.

You ask me to speak but my mouth
holds back—my heart
a house God remodels daily
with an axe.

You who say my mouth belongs
to someone else.

Lay me low, sweet chariot.

The walks we took led us nowhere,
only deeper in.

My mouth full of nettles, your hair
crowned with seeds
parachuting towards the earth
in some recurring dream

where you appear, my husband
taking notes beside our bed
as I mumble in my sleep about a snake
that has come between us . . .

Marriage a tapestry full of holes
hanging in a castle with the drawbridge
permanently up—
                               its faithful servants
unable to repair the wormage

in the lower left hand corner.

SINE QUA NON

Your husband is your future, he says;
I'm from your distant past, something

on a shelf to look at. I look him over
the way one looks at a German viola

made in 1768, once snubbed for not
being Italian, now safely displayed

behind glass. My violist. I look at him
and say: *You of all people must know*

the joy in dusting off that instrument,
restringing the thing, then making it

sound again—a sound like no other.

THE LOVERS

I was always afraid
of the next card

the psychic would turn
over for us—
                    Forgive me
for not knowing
how we were

every card in the deck.

UNSLEEPING, 5:36 A.M.

Neither high-flying kite nor
the hand that holds it. Neither
parent nor grandparent, glass
of cold milk nor cookies straight
out of the oven. We are double
domiciled—golden beeswax
columns crowned with guttering
flames amidst the comings
and goings. It took my entire life
to find you inside this garden
without walls, my body leaning
into yours more like paradise
than bedding down anyone else
within reach. Rapt and raptor,
we are the fruit of twin trees—
order and chaos, the forbidden
and the blessed—forms of time
unable to contain eternity's
drunken spark that leapt out of
the void and set the heavens in
motion, cooking up whatever's
not on the menu even if it means
burning down the kitchen in order
to let the winter stars back in—
the Southern Cross sailing across
a sky swathed in rosy light—
raptors circling above a cradle
made out of mud and twigs,
winged chorus of ecstasy and fear
singing what's known by heart.

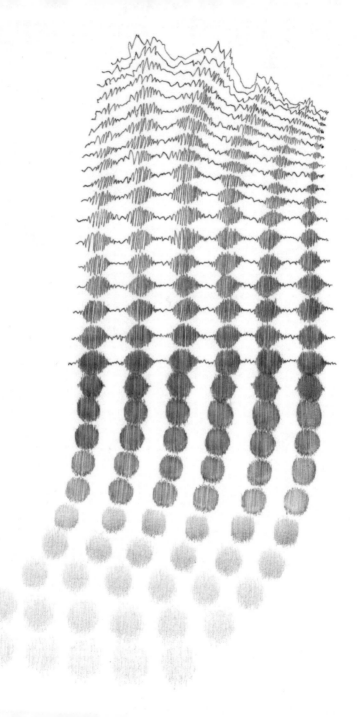

THE REMAINS

—*Wuxi, China*

Walking out of the new cemetery, my father
takes my hand, having just re-interred the remains
of his own father and his father's two wives—
his mother dead from T.B. by the time he was ten.

He takes my hand and says, *Now I can die in peace*
even if we didn't get the actual bones. Village thugs
hired by my uncle made sure the burial mounds
behind the house my father grew up in would not feel

a single shovel blade go in as they stood there
sentinel with arms crossed. My uncle's wife
had a dream that out of the grave's opened gash
demons rushed—ancestral ghosts not wanting to be

disturbed. *In less than a decade, bulldozers will come*
to take the Liu village down. My grandfather's
ashes, my grandmother's bones, my own father
walking away with two fistfuls of dirt and saying,

This will have to do. So many others have died
who've left nothing behind. I'll never come back
to this place again. My father kisses my hand,
I who've flown across twelve time zones to be here

at his side in a borrowed van, me looking out
the window at a countryside once overrun
with Japs marching West along the railroad tracks,
my father and his siblings hiding in an outhouse,

a dead horse found in the schoolyard soon after
the soldiers had gone. Your hands are so soft! I say
to my father. *So are yours*, he says. *Remember
when it was we last held hands?* I must have been

a kid, I say, maybe eight, or ten? *You were six*,
my father says. And I'm still your son, I say,
leaning into his shoulder, our hands the same size.
And I'll always be your father, my father says

before I have the chance to say another word,
my eighty-year-old father nodding off into sleep.

Winners of the Saturnalia Books Poetry Prize:

Thieves in the Afterlife by Kendra DeColo

Lullaby (with Exit Sign) by Hadara Bar-Nadav

My Scarlet Ways by Tanya Larkin

The Little Office of the Immaculate Conception by Martha Silano

Personification by Margaret Ronda

To the Bone by Sebastian Agudelo

Famous Last Words by Catherine Pierce

Dummy Fire by Sarah Vap

Correspondence by Kathleen Graber

The Babies by Sabrina Orah Mark

Also Available from saturnalia books:

That Our Eyes Be Rigged by Kristi Maxwell

Reckless Lovelys by Martha Silano

A spell of songs by Peter Jay Shippy

Each Chartered Street by Sebastian Agudelo

No Object by Natalie Shapero

Nowhere Fast by William Kulik

Arco Iris by Sarah Vap

The Girls of Peculiar by Catherine Pierce

Xing by Debora Kuan

Other Romes by Derek Mong

Faulkner's Rosary by Sarah Vap

Gurlesque: the new grrly, grotesque, burlesque poetics edited by Lara Glenum and Arielle Greenberg

Tsim Tsum by Sabrina Orah Mark

Hush Sessions by Kristi Maxwell

Days of Unwilling by Cal Bedient

Letters to Poets: Conversations about Poetics, Politics, and Community
edited by Jennifer Firestone and Dana Teen Lomax

Artist/Poet Collaboration Series:

Velleity's Shade by Star Black / Artwork by Bill Knott
Polytheogamy by Timothy Liu / Artwork by Greg Drasler
Midnights by Jane Miller / Artwork by Beverly Pepper
Stigmata Errata Etcetera by Bill Knott / Artwork by Star Black
Ing Grish by John Yau / Artwork by Thomas Nozkowski
Blackboards by Tomaz Salamun / Artwork by Metka Krasovec

Don't Go Back to Sleep was printed using the fonts Trajan Pro and Adobe Garamond Pro.

www.saturnaliabooks.org